Illustrations © Copyright 2017

All rights reserved.

THANK YOU!

THANK YOU FOR PURCHASING THE BOOK. PLAYHOUSE TAKES PRIDE IN PROVIDING THE BEST COLLECTION OF BOOKS FOR CHILDREN. WE WELCOME ALL FEEDBACK AND SUGGESTIONS SO PLEASE FEEL FREE TO LEAVE A REVIEW OF THE BOOK ON AMAZON.

Riddle:

The more you take away, the larger it gets? What is it?

ANSWER ON NEXT PAGE!

Answer:

A hole.

Riddle:

Which type of vehicle is spelled the same forwards and backwards?

ANSWER ON NEXT PAGE!

Answer:

Racecar.

Riddle:

What is yours, but others use it more than you do?

ANSWER ON NEXT PAGE!

Answer:

Your name.

Riddle:

What's the easiest way to make an octopus laugh?

ANSWER ON NEXT PAGE!

Answer:

Ten-tickles.

Riddle:

Two fathers and two sons went fishing together. Everyone caught a fish, there were 3 fish in total. How is this possible?

ANSWER ON NEXT PAGE!

Answer:

There were only 3 people. A grandfather, a father, and a grandson.

Riddle:

What kind of coat can be put on only when wet?

ANSWER ON NEXT PAGE!

Answer:

A coat of paint.

Riddle:

You draw a line. Now how do you make the line longer without touching it?

ANSWER ON NEXT PAGE!

Answer:

Draw a shorter line next to it, and it becomes a longer line.

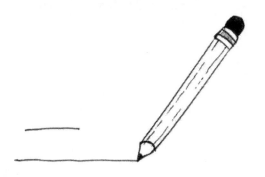

Riddle:

How can you physically stand behind your friend as your friend physically stands behind you?

ANSWER ON NEXT PAGE!

Answer:

Standing back to back.

Riddle:

People buy me to eat,
but never eat me.
What am I?

ANSWER ON NEXT PAGE!

Answer:

A plate.

Riddle:

What has eighty-eight keys but cannot open a single door?

ANSWER ON NEXT PAGE!

Answer:

A piano.

Riddle:

If a rooster lays an egg on a rounded roof which way does it roll?

ANSWER ON NEXT PAGE!

Answer:

Roosters don't lay eggs.

Riddle:

What loses a head in the morning and gets it back at night?

ANSWER ON NEXT PAGE!

Answer:

A pillow.

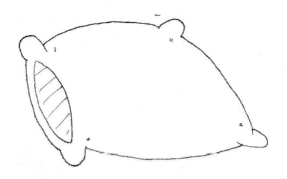

Riddle:

You throw away the outside and cook the inside. Then you eat just the outside and throw away the inside. What did you eat?

ANSWER ON NEXT PAGE!

Answer:

Corn on the cob.

Riddle:

It has a bark, but does not bite. What is it?

ANSWER ON NEXT PAGE!

Answer:

A tree.

Riddle:

How can you drop a raw egg onto a concrete floor without cracking it?

ANSWER ON NEXT PAGE!

Answer:

The concrete floor will not crack because of a raw egg.

Riddle:

Before Mt. Everest was discovered as the tallest mountain in the world, which mountain was the tallest?

ANSWER ON NEXT PAGE!

Answer:

Mt Everest.

Riddle:

What are moving left to right, right now?

ANSWER ON NEXT PAGE!

Answer:

Your eyes.

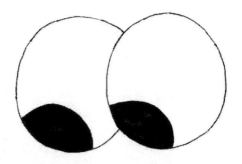

Riddle:

I'm tall when I'm young,
short when I'm old.
What am I?

ANSWER ON NEXT PAGE!

Answer:

A candle.

Riddle:

What has no beginning,
end, or middle?

ANSWER ON NEXT PAGE!

Answer:

A doughnut.

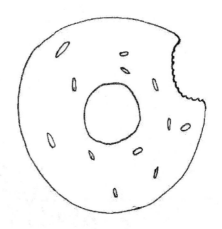

Riddle:

When is a doctor most angry?

ANSWER ON NEXT PAGE!

Answer:

When he is out of patients.

Riddle:

When does Christmas come before Thanksgiving?

ANSWER ON NEXT PAGE!

Answer:

In a dictionary.

Riddle:

When an elephant sits on your fence, what time is it?

ANSWER ON NEXT PAGE!

Answer:

Time to buy a new fence.

Riddle:

What fruit has seeds on the outside?

ANSWER ON NEXT PAGE!

Answer:

A strawberry.

Riddle:

David was out for a walk and it started to rain. He did not have an umbrella and he wasn't wearing a hat. His clothes got soaked, yet not a single hair on David's head got wet.

ANSWER ON NEXT PAGE!

Answer:

David was bald.

Riddle:

A man jumps out of 15-story building and lands on solid concrete. The man was not injured. How can this be?

ANSWER ON NEXT PAGE!

Answer:

The man jumped from the first story

Riddle:

A cowboy rode into a town on Friday. He stayed two nights and left on Friday. How could that be?

ANSWER ON NEXT PAGE!

Answer:

His horses name was Friday.

Riddle:

If an electric train is travelling north, which way will the smoke go?

ANSWER ON NEXT PAGE!

Answer:

There is no smoke; it is an electric train!

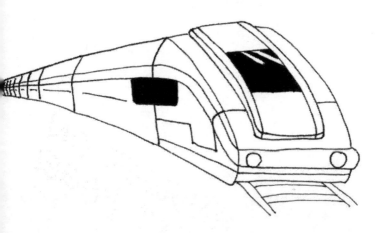

Riddle:

When it rains, what goes up?

ANSWER ON NEXT PAGE!

Answer:

An umbrella.

Riddle:

If you have three you have three, if you have two you have two and if you have one you have none. What am I?

ANSWER ON NEXT PAGE!

Answer:

Choices.

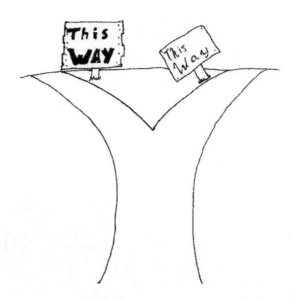

Riddle:

What has 4 fingers and a thumb, but is not living?

ANSWER ON NEXT PAGE!

Answer:

A glove.

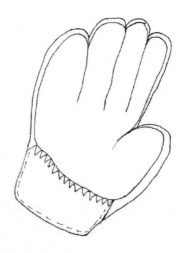

Riddle:

Which weighs more, a pound of feathers or a pound of bricks?

ANSWER ON NEXT PAGE!

Answer:

They both weigh one pound.

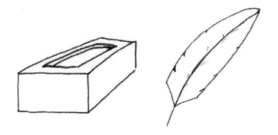

Riddle:

How can you make seven even?

ANSWER ON NEXT PAGE!

Answer:

Remove the "s".

Riddle:

What do you put in a barrel to make it lighter?

ANSWER ON NEXT PAGE!

Answer:

A hole.

Riddle:

What travels around the world but stays in one corner?

ANSWER ON NEXT PAGE!

Answer:

A stamp.

Riddle:

What gets whiter the dirtier it gets?

ANSWER ON NEXT PAGE!

Answer:

A chalkboard.

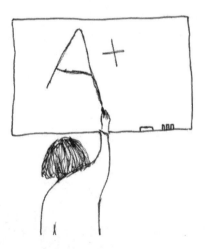

Riddle:

What kind of room has no windows or doors?

ANSWER ON NEXT PAGE!

Answer:

A mushroom.

Riddle:

If there are 3 apples and you take away 2, how many do you have?

ANSWER ON NEXT PAGE!

Answer:

You will have 2 apples.

Riddle:

What is brown and sticky?

ANSWER ON NEXT PAGE!

Answer:

A stick!

Riddle:

A boy is walking down the road with a doctor. While the boy is the doctor's son, the doctor isn't the boy's father. Who is the doctor?

ANSWER ON NEXT PAGE!

Answer:

The boy's mother.

Riddle:

You answer me, but I never ask you a question. What am I?

ANSWER ON NEXT PAGE!

Answer:

A telephone.

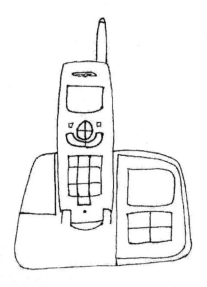

Riddle:

No matter how much rain comes down, it won't get any wetter.

ANSWER ON NEXT PAGE!

Answer:

Water.

Riddle:

What runs around the yard without moving?

ANSWER ON NEXT PAGE!

Answer:

A fence.

Riddle:

What's full of holes but still holds water?

ANSWER ON NEXT PAGE!

Answer:

A sponge.

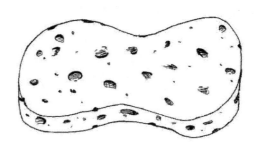

Riddle:

What is more useful
when broken?

ANSWER ON NEXT PAGE!

Answer:

An egg.

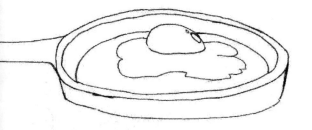

Riddle:

What can jump higher than a building?

ANSWER ON NEXT PAGE!

Answer:

Anything that jumps. Buildings cannot jump.

Riddle:

What gets wetter
as it dries?

ANSWER ON NEXT PAGE!

Answer:

A towel.

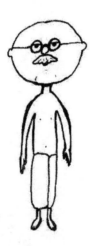

Riddle:

What has two hands
and a face?

ANSWER ON NEXT PAGE!

Answer:

A clock.

Riddle:

What begins with t, ends with t and has t in it?

ANSWER ON NEXT PAGE!

Answer:

A teapot.

Riddle:

A baseball glove and a ball cost $1.10 in total. The glove costs $1.00 more than the ball. How much does the ball cost?

ANSWER ON NEXT PAGE!

Answer:

A nickel ($0.05).

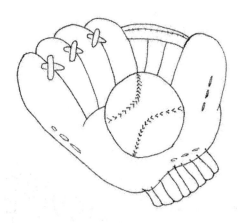

Riddle:

What can you catch
but not throw?

ANSWER ON NEXT PAGE!

Answer:

A cold.

Riddle:

The more you take, the more you leave behind. What are they?

ANSWER ON NEXT PAGE!

Answer:

Footprints.

Riddle:

What can fly around all day but never goes anywhere?

ANSWER ON NEXT PAGE!

Answer:

A flag.

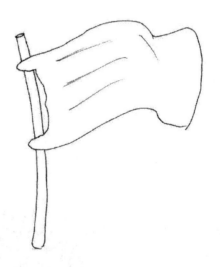

Riddle:

A kind of tree can you carry in your hand?

ANSWER ON NEXT PAGE!

Answer:

A palm tree.

Riddle:

What can you hold,
without ever using
your hands?

ANSWER ON NEXT PAGE!

Answer:

Your breath.

Riddle:

What has a head and tail, but no body?

ANSWER ON NEXT PAGE!

Answer:

A coin.

Riddle:

What has an eye but cannot see?

ANSWER ON NEXT PAGE!

Answer:

A needle.

Riddle:

What has four wheels and flies?

ANSWER ON NEXT PAGE!

Answer:

A garbage truck.

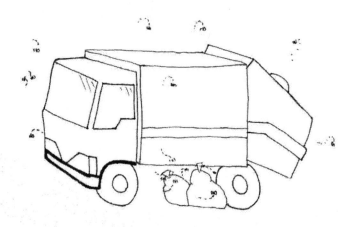

Riddle:

People need me, however they always give me away.
What am I?

ANSWER ON NEXT PAGE!

Answer:

Money.

Riddle:

What has four legs,
but can't walk?

ANSWER ON NEXT PAGE!

Answer:

A table.

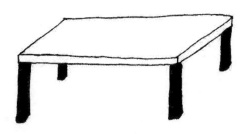

Riddle:

Why are teddy bears never hungry?

ANSWER ON NEXT PAGE!

Answer:

Because they are always stuffed.

Riddle:

What is at the end
of a rainbow?

ANSWER ON NEXT PAGE!

Answer:

The letter "w".

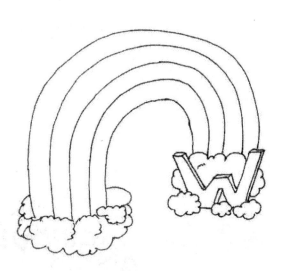

Riddle:

How can you throw a ball 10 meters, and have it come back to you without hitting anything?

ANSWER ON NEXT PAGE!

Answer:

Throw the ball straight up.

Riddle:

What can run but never walk?

ANSWER ON NEXT PAGE!

Answer:

Water.

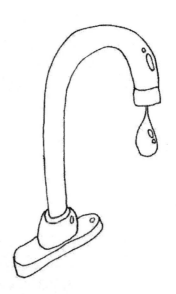

Riddle:

Imagine you're in a room that is filling with water. There are no windows or doors. How do you get out?

ANSWER ON NEXT PAGE!

Answer:

Stop imagining.

Riddle:

What has a neck
but no head?

ANSWER ON NEXT PAGE!

Answer:

A bottle.

Riddle:

How can a man go eight days without sleep?

ANSWER ON NEXT PAGE!

Answer:

By sleeping at night.

Riddle:

What grows when it eats, but dies when it drinks?

ANSWER ON NEXT PAGE!

Answer:

Fire.

Riddle:

How many bricks does it take to complete a building made of brick?

ANSWER ON NEXT PAGE!

Answer:

One brick
(The last one).

Riddle:

Who can shave 20 times a day and still have a beard?

ANSWER ON NEXT PAGE!

Answer:

A barber.

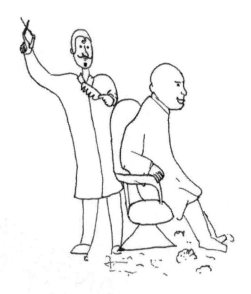

Riddle:

What's the strongest animal in the world?

ANSWER ON NEXT PAGE!

Answer:

A Snail.

They carry their house on their back.

Riddle:

What goes through towns and over hills but never moves?

ANSWER ON NEXT PAGE!

Answer:

A road.

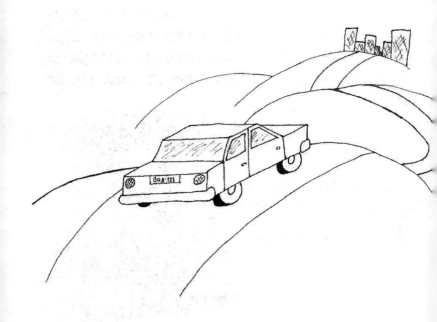

THANK YOU!

We hope you enjoyed the book. If you have any comments/questions or simply want to provide some feedback, please feel free to leave a review on Amazon. Any feedback is greatly appreciated.

If you enjoyed this book, you can get a free copy of *101 Riddles by* PlayHouse. A riddle book containing intermediate difficulty riddles. Fun and challenging for the whole family!

https://playhousepublishing.wixsite.com/freeoffer

Made in the USA
San Bernardino, CA
14 December 2018